Ward Lock Educational Storyworld
General Editor: Geoffrey Summerfield

Scottish Highland Tales

Scottish Highland Tales

Selected by Iain Crichton Smith
Ward Lock Educational

Ling Kee

WARD LOCK EDUCATIONAL CO., LTD.
47 MARYLEBONE LANE,
LONDON W1M 6AX

A member of the Ling Kee Group
LONDON · HONG KONG · TAIPEI

Series advisers:
Ralph Lavender and Dennis Saunders

SCOTTISH HIGHLAND TALES
First published 1982

ISBN 0 7062 3948 2 school edition
ISBN 0 7062 3952 0 net edition

This collection © Iain Crichton Smith 1982

The *Seal Woman* story is based on a version published by the School of Scottish Studies, University of Edinburgh, in *Tocher* 8, pp. 258–63, and appears by consent of the Director of the School and the Editor of *Tocher*. The original recording was made in 1968 by Mr A. J. MacDonald from Mr Donald MacDougall, Struan Ruadh, North Uist.

The *Three Shirts* story is based on a version published by the School of Scottish Studies, University of Edinburgh in *Tocher* 2, pp. 38–57, and appears by consent of the Director of the School and the Editor of *Tocher*. The original recording was made in 1969 by Mr A. J. MacDonald from the late Mr D. A. Johnson, Ardmore, South Uist.

PRINTED BY TOPMAN PRINTING PRESS LTD.

Contents

Photographs on pages 2/3, 6 and 36
by Christopher Locke, on page 58 by Eliott Erwitt
and on page 96 by Fay Godwin
Flicker book by Tony Watson

The Battle of the Birds

There was once a time when every animal and bird
was gathering to fight a battle. The son of the King
of Tethertown said that he would go and see the
battle, and that he would bring sure word home to
his father who would be king of the creatures that
year. The battle was over when he arrived but for
one fight between a big black raven and a snake, and
it seemed as if the snake would beat the raven.
When the King's son saw this, he helped the raven
and with one blow took off the snake's head. When
the raven had got his breath back and saw that the
snake was dead, he said to the King's son, 'For your
kindness to me this day I will show you a great
sight. Come on up now on the root of my two
wings.' The King's son climbed up on the raven and
the bird took him over seven bens, seven glens and
seven mountain moors.

'Now,' said the raven, 'do you see that house over
there? Go to it. It is a sister of mine that stays in it:
and I assure you that she will make you very
welcome. And if she asks you, "Were you at the
battle of the birds?" say that you were and if she
asks, "Did you see the raven there?" say that you did.
But be sure that you meet me early tomorrow
morning in this place.' The King's son was well
treated that night, as had been foretold by the raven,
with the best of food, the best of drink, warm water
for his feet and a soft bed for his limbs.

On the next day the raven showed him the same
sight as before – seven bens, seven glens and seven

mountain moors. They saw a cottage far off but though it was far they were soon there. Again the King's son got good treatment, as he had done the night before, with plenty of food and drink, and warm water for his feet and a soft bed for his limbs.

On the third morning instead of seeing the raven, who should meet him but the handsomest lad he had ever seen, with a bundle in his hand. The King's son asked this lad if he had seen a big black raven. The lad said to him, 'You will never see that raven again for I am the raven. I was put under a spell: it was meeting you that freed me and for that you are getting this bundle. Now,' said the lad, 'you will turn back the way you came and you will stay a night in each house as you did before: but you must not loose the bundle that I gave you, till you are in the place where you would most like to dwell.'

The King's son turned his back to the lad and his face to his father's house: and he got lodging from the raven's sisters, just as he had got it before when he was on his way forward. When he was nearing his father's house he was passing through a dense wood. It seemed to him that the bundle was growing heavy and he thought he would have a look to see what was in it.

When he opened the bundle he was greatly
astonished for in a twinkling he saw the grandest
place he had ever seen, with a great castle and an
orchard about the castle in which was every kind of
fruit and herb. He stood there full of wonder and
regret for having opened the bundle which it was
not now in his power to close again: and he would
have wished this pretty place to be in the beautiful
green hollow that was opposite his father's house.

At that very moment he saw a great giant coming
towards him.

'You have built your house in a bad place, King's
son,' said the giant.

'Yes, but it is not here I would wish it to be,' said
the King's son, 'though it happened to be here by ill
luck.'

'What reward would you give me for putting it
back in the bundle as it was before?' asked the giant.

'What reward would you ask?' said the King's son.

'If you will give me the first son you have when
he is seven years of age,' said the giant, 'I will put the
bundle back.'

'If I have a son you shall have him,' said the
King's son. In a twinkling the giant put the orchard
and castle in the bundle as before.

'Now,' said the giant, 'you take your own road
and I will take mine. But remember your promise
and though you may forget I shall remember.'

The King's son took to the road and at the end of
a few days he reached the place he was fondest of.
He opened the bundle, and the castle and orchard
appeared just as before. And when he opened the

castle door he saw the most beautiful maiden he had ever cast eyes upon.

'Come,' said the pretty maiden, 'everything is in order for you if you will marry me this night.'

'I am certainly willing to do that,' said the King's son. And on the same night they married and became King and Queen. And nine months afterwards they had a handsome baby son.

At the end of seven years and a day, what big man was seen coming to the castle but the giant? The new King remembered his promise to him, though till now he had not told it to his wife. However when he did tell her, she said, 'You leave this matter between me and the giant.'

'Turn out your son,' said the giant. 'Remember your promise.'

'You will get him,' said the King, 'when his mother has prepared him for his journey.'

The new Queen arrayed the cook's son and gave him to the giant by the hand. The giant went away with him but he had not gone far when he put a rod in the little lad's hand.

The giant asked him, 'If your father had that rod, what would he do with it?'

'If my father had that rod,' said the little lad, 'he would beat the dogs and the cats, if they went near the King's meat.'

'You are the cook's son,' said the giant angrily and turned back to the castle in rage and madness; and he shouted to the King that if he did not turn out his son to him, the highest stone of the castle would be the lowest.

The Queen then said to the King, 'We will try it again: the butler's son is the same age as ours.'

She arrayed the butler's son and she gave him to the giant by the hand. The giant had not gone far when he put the rod in the little lad's hand.

'If your father had that rod,' said the giant, 'what would he do with it?'

'He would beat the dogs and the cats when they came near the King's bottles and glasses.'

'You are the butler's son,' said the giant angrily and returned to the castle in great rage and madness. The earth shook under the soles of his feet and the castle and all that was in it shook as well.

'OUT HERE WITH YOUR SON,' said the giant, 'or in a twinkling the stone that is highest in the dwelling will be the lowest.'

So the King and the Queen had to give their son to the giant. And the giant took him to his own house and reared him as his own son.

One day when the giant was away from home the lad heard the sweetest music he had ever heard coming from a room at the top of the giant's house. When he opened the door he saw at a glance the most beautiful girl he had ever seen. She beckoned him to come nearer to her and she told him to go away this time but to be sure to return on the stroke of midnight.

The lad kept his word and the giant's daughter was at his side in a twinkling and said, 'Tomorrow you will get the choice of my two sisters to marry: but say that you will not take either, but me. My father wants me to marry the King of the Green City but I don't like him.'

On the following day the giant took out his three daughters and said,

'Now, son of the King of Tethertown, you have not lost anything by living with me so long. You will get as your wife one of my two eldest daughters and permission to go home with her the day after the wedding.'

'If you will give me this pretty little one,' said the King's son, 'I will take you at your word.'

The giant's anger kindled and he said, 'Before you get her you must do the three things that I ask you to do.'

'Say on,' said the King's son.

The giant took him to the byre.

'Now,' said he, 'the dung of a hundred cattle is

here and it has not been cleansed for seven years. I am going away from home today and if this byre is not cleaned before night comes, so clean that a golden apple will run from end to end of it, not only will you not get my daughter but it will be a drink of your blood that will quench my thirst tonight.'

The King's son began cleaning the byre but he might just as well have been baling the great ocean. After midday when sweat was blinding him the giant's young daughter came and said to him, 'You are being punished, King's son.'

'I am that,' he replied.

'Come over here,' she said, 'and rest.'

'I will do that,' he said. 'There is but death waiting for me at any rate.'

He sat down near her and was so tired that he fell asleep beside her. When he awoke the giant's daughter was not to be seen, but the byre was so well cleaned that a golden apple would run from end to end of it.

In came the giant and said, 'Have you cleaned the byre, King's son?'

'I have cleaned it,' he answered.

'Somebody cleaned it,' said the giant.

'You did not clean it anyway,' said the King's son.

'Well, well,' said the giant, 'since you worked so hard today you will go this time tomorrow and thatch this byre with birds' down but with no two feathers of one colour.'

The King's son was afoot before the sun. He caught up his bow and quiver of arrows to kill the birds. He took to the moors but though he did so

the birds were not so easy to catch. He was running after them till the sweat was blinding him.

After midday who should come but the giant's daughter.

'You are exhausting yourself,' she said.

'I am,' he said. 'There fell only these two blackbirds and as you can see they are both of the one colour.'

'Come and rest on this pretty hillock,' said the giant's daughter.

'I am very willing to do that,' he said. He thought she would help him this time too and he sat down near her and he was not long there till he fell asleep. When he awoke the giant's daughter was gone.

He thought he would go back to the house and when he got there he saw that the byre had been thatched with feathers.

When the giant came home he said, 'Have you thatched the byre, King's son?'

'I thatched it,' he said.

'Somebody thatched it,' said the giant.

'You didn't thatch it anyway,' said the King's son.

'Well, well,' said the giant, 'there is a fir tree beside that loch down there and there is a magpie's nest at the top. You will find eggs in the nest. I must have them for my first meal. Not one must be burst or broken, and there are five in the nest.'

Early in the morning the King's son went where the tree was and it was not hard to find for there was none like it in the wood. From the base of the tree to the first branch was five hundred feet. The King's son was going all round the tree when the giant's daughter (she who was always bringing help to him) came.

'You are losing the skin of your hands and feet,' she said.

'I know,' he said. 'No sooner do I climb up than I fall down.'

'This is no time for stopping,' said the giant's daughter.

She thrust finger after finger into the tree till she had made a ladder for the King's son to climb up to the magpie's nest.

When he was at the nest she said, 'Make haste now with the eggs for my father's breath is burning my back.'

Because of his hurry she left her little finger in the top of the tree. 'Now,' she said, 'you will go home with the eggs quickly and you will marry me tonight if you can recognize me. I and my two sisters will be arrayed in the same garments, and we will look like each other, but glance at me when my father says "Go to your wife, King's son" and you will see a hand without a little finger.'

The King's son gave the eggs to the giant, and the giant told him, 'Make ready for your marriage.'

Then indeed there was a wedding and what a wedding! There were giants and gentlemen and the son of the King of the Green City was in the midst of them. The dancing began and what a dance it was. The giant's house was shaking from top to bottom. When bedtime came the giant said, 'It is time for you to go to your bed, son of the King of Tethertown: take your bride with you from among those.' And he pointed towards this three daughters, who were all dressed alike. The younger daughter put out the hand with the missing finger and the King's son caught her by the hand.

'You have done well, this time,' said the giant, 'but perhaps you won't be so lucky next time.'

And the King's son and his wife went to bed. 'Now,' she said, 'do not sleep or else you will die. We must fly quickly, quickly, or for certain my father will kill you.'

Out they went and mounted the blue-grey horse in the stable.

'Stop awhile,' she said, 'and I will play a trick on the old fellow.' She went back into the house and cut an apple into nine pieces, and she put two pieces at the head of the bed, and two pieces at the foot of the bed, and two pieces at the door of the kitchen, and two pieces at the big door and one outside the house.

The giant awoke and called out, 'Are you asleep?'

'We are not yet,' said the apple that was at the head of the bed. After a while the giant called again.

'We are not yet,' said the apple that was at the foot of the bed.

A while after this he called again.

'We are not yet,' said the apple at the kitchen door.

The giant called again and this time the apple that was at the big door answered.

'You are going further from me,' said the giant.

'We are not yet,' said the apple that was outside the house.

'You are moving away from me,' said the giant and he jumped to his feet and to the bed he went but it was cold and empty. 'My daughter's tricks are testing me,' said the giant. And he went after them.

At dawn the giant's daughter said that her father's breath was burning her back.

'Put your hand quickly,' she said to the King's son, 'in the ear of the grey horse and whatever you find in it throw it behind you.'

'There is a twig of a sloe tree,' he said.

'Throw it behind you,' she said.

No sooner had he done so than there were twenty miles of blackthorn wood, so thick that scarcely a weasel could go through it. The giant came at a headlong pace and landed with his head and neck in the thorns.

'My own daughter's tricks are as bad as ever,' he said, 'but if I had my big axe and wood knife here I would not be long making a way through this wood.' He went home for the big axe and the wood knife and he was not long on his journey. When he returned he was not long in making a path through the wood with them.

'I will leave the wood knife and the axe here till I return,' said the giant.

'If you leave them,' said a hoodie that was in the tree, 'we will steal them.'

'I'm sure you would do that,' said the giant,
'and I had better take them home.' He returned
and left them at the house.

In the heat of the day the giant's daughter felt
her father's breath burning her back. She said to
her husband, 'Put your finger in the horse's ear and
throw behind you whatever you find in it.' The
King's son found a splinter of grey stone and in a
twinkling there were twenty miles of great grey
rock behind them. The giant came full pelt, but past
the rock he could not go.

'The tricks of my daughter are the hardest things
that I have ever met,' said the giant, 'but if I had my
lever and my mighty mattock I would not be long
making my way through this as well.' There was no
help for it but to go back for them. He did so and
he was not long in making a road through the
rock with them.

'I will leave the tools here and return no more,' he said.

'If you leave them,' said the hoodie, 'we will steal them.'

'Do that if you want,' said the giant, 'there is no time to go back.'

In the twilight the giant's daughter said that she was feeling her father's breath burning her back.

'Look in the horse's ear, King's son,' she said, 'or else we are lost.'

He did as she told him and it was a bladder of
water that he found in the horse's ear this time. He
threw it behind him and suddenly there was a fresh-
water loch, twenty miles in length and breadth,
behind them.

The giant came on but his speed was so great that
he ended up in the middle of the loch and he went
under and he rose no more.

On the next day the King's son and his bride
came in sight of his father's house.

'Now,' said she, 'my father is drowned and he
won't trouble us any more. But before we go
further you go to your father's house and tell him
that you have me with you. But remember, let
neither man nor creature kiss you for if they do you
will not remember that you have ever seen me.'

Everyone he met welcomed him and he told his
father and mother not to kiss him, but as ill luck
would have it an old greyhound was in the house
and she knew him and jumped up to his mouth and
after that he did not remember the giant's daughter.

She sat at the side of the well where he had left
her but the King's son did not come. In the evening
she climbed up into an oak tree that was beside the
well, and lay in the fork of the tree all that night.

A shoemaker had a house near the well and about
midday on the following day he asked his wife to
fetch him a drink from it. When the shoemaker's
wife reached the well, and saw the reflection of the
girl that was up in the tree, she thought it was her
own reflection: and as she had never before thought
that she was so beautiful she dashed the dish that she
had in her hand onto the ground and went back to
the house without vessel or water.

'Where is the water, wife?' said the shoemaker.

'You shambling contemptible graceless old man,'
she replied. 'I have stayed too long as your wood
and water slave.'

'I think, wife, that you have gone crazy.
Daughter, you go and fetch a drink for your father.'

His daughter went and the same thing happened
to her. She never thought that she was so beautiful,
and she returned home without vessel or water.

'Give me the drink,' said her father.

'You home-spun old shoemaker,' she said, 'do
you think that I am going to be your water slave?'

The poor shoemaker thought that they had both
gone crazy and he went himself to the well.

He saw the reflection of the maiden there and he looked up to the tree and he saw the most beautiful woman he had ever seen.

'Your seat is unsteady but your face is lovely,' said the shoemaker. 'Come down, for I need you for a short while at my house.'

The shoemaker understood that this was the reflection that had made his wife and daughter crazy.

The shoemaker took the giant's daughter to his house and he said that he had but a poor cottage but that she should get a share of all that was in it.

At the end of a day or two there came a group of young gentlemen to the shoemaker's house for shoes to be made them, for the King's son had come home and he was going to marry.

When the lads glanced at the giant's daughter they thought they had never seen anyone as pretty as she.

'You certainly have a beautiful daughter there,' they said to the shoemaker.

'She is beautiful indeed,' said the shoemaker, 'but she is no daughter of mine.'

'By Saint Nail,' said one of them, 'I would give a hundred pounds to marry her.'

And the two others said the same. The poor shoemaker said that he had nothing to do with her. 'But,' they said, 'you ask her about marriage tonight and send us word tomorrow.'

When the gentlemen had gone away, she asked the shoemaker, 'What was that they were saying about me?' The shoemaker told her.

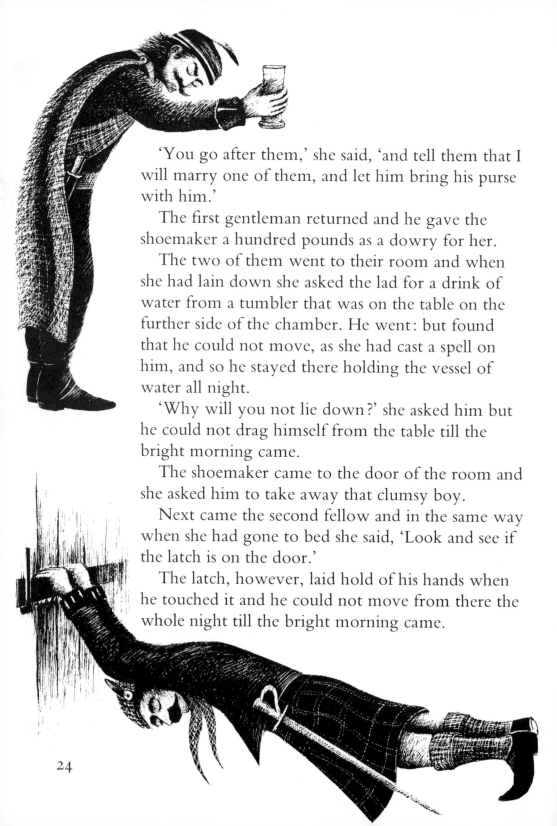

'You go after them,' she said, 'and tell them that I will marry one of them, and let him bring his purse with him.'

The first gentleman returned and he gave the shoemaker a hundred pounds as a dowry for her.

The two of them went to their room and when she had lain down she asked the lad for a drink of water from a tumbler that was on the table on the further side of the chamber. He went: but found that he could not move, as she had cast a spell on him, and so he stayed there holding the vessel of water all night.

'Why will you not lie down?' she asked him but he could not drag himself from the table till the bright morning came.

The shoemaker came to the door of the room and she asked him to take away that clumsy boy.

Next came the second fellow and in the same way when she had gone to bed she said, 'Look and see if the latch is on the door.'

The latch, however, laid hold of his hands when he touched it and he could not move from there the whole night till the bright morning came.

No matter, he did not tell the other two what had
happened to him, because he was so ashamed of
being tricked: and on the third night the last one
came.

The same thing that had happened to the first two
happened to him. One of his feet stuck to the floor
and he could not move, and he stood like that all
night.

In the morning he too left that place, and he did
not look behind him.

'Now,' said the girl to the shoemaker, 'the
sporran of gold belongs to you: I have no need of it.
It will help you and I will not miss it, and I give it to
you for your kindness to me.'

The shoemaker had the shoes ready for the young
gentlemen and on that very day the King's son was
to be married. He was taking the shoes to the castle

when the girl said to him, 'I would like to see the King's son before he gets married.'

'Come with me,' said the shoemaker. 'I am well acquainted with the servants at the castle and you will see the King's son and all the company.'

When the gentlemen saw the pretty girl, they took her to the wedding-room and they filled a glass with wine for her. When she was going to drink what was in the glass, a flame suddenly came from it, and a golden pigeon and a silver one sprang out.

They were flying about when three grains of barley fell on the floor. The silver pigeon ate them and the golden pigeon said to him,

'If you had remembered the time I cleaned the byre you would not eat all that without giving me a share.'

Three other grains of barley fell and the silver pigeon ate them as before.

'If you had remembered the time I thatched the byre you would not eat all that without giving me a share,' said the golden pigeon.

Three other grains fell and the silver pigeon ate them.

'If you had remembered when I pillaged the magpie's nest,' said the golden pigeon, 'you would not eat all that without giving me a share. I lost my little finger when you were climbing to it, and I want it back.'

Then the King's son remembered, and he knew who the girl was. He sprang towards her and kissed her from her hand to her mouth and the priest was sent for and they were married for the second time. And they lived happily ever after.

The Hoodie

There was once a farmer who had four daughters. They were washing clothes at a river when a hoodie came round and said to the eldest one:

'Will you marry me, farmer's daughter?'

'I will not, you ugly brute. An ugly brute is the hoodie,' she said.

On the following day he came to the second daughter and said to her,

'Will you marry me?'

'Not me,' she said, 'an ugly brute is the hoodie.'

On the third day he came to the third daughter and said to her,

'Will you marry me?'

'Not me,' she said, 'an ugly brute is the hoodie.'

On the fourth day he said to the youngest
daughter,
'Will you marry me?'
'I will marry you,' she said, 'a pretty creature is
the hoodie.'
And on the following day they were married.
The hoodie said to her, 'Would you rather that I
was a hoodie by day and a man by night: or a hoodie
by night and a man by day?'

'I would rather you were a man by day and a hoodie by night,' she said.

After this he was a splendid fellow by day and a hoodie by night.

A few days after they were married he took her with him to his own house.

At the end of nine months they had a son. In the night there came the most beautiful music that was ever heard and while everyone slept the child was taken away. When the child's father came to the house in the morning to find out how they all were he was very sad that the child had been taken away, for fear that he should be blamed for it himself.

At the end of another nine months they had another son. This time a watch was set on the house. But the beautiful music came as before, everyone slept, and the child was taken away. When the child's father came to the house in the morning to find out if everything was as it should be, he was told that the child had been taken away, and he did not know what to do for sorrow.

Again at the end of nine months they had another son. A watch was set on the house as usual, but the music came about the house as before, everyone slept, and the child was taken away.

When they rose on the following day they went to another house that they had, himself, his wife and her three sisters. On the way he said to them, 'See that you have not forgotten anything.'

His wife said, 'I forgot my comb,' and suddenly the coach in which they were travelling became a withered faggot, and her husband became a hoodie again and flew away.

Her sisters returned home but she followed the hoodie. When she caught sight of him on a hilltop she would follow him in order to try and catch him: but whenever she reached the top of the hill he would be in a hollow on the other side. When night came she was tired and she had no place in which to rest or stay. She saw a little house of light far from her, but though it was far she did not take long to reach it.

When she arrived she stood wretchedly at the
door. She saw a little lad in the house and she liked
him very much. The woman of the house told her
to come in and said that she knew the purpose of her
journey. She was given a bed for the night but no
sooner did the day come than she rose. She went out
and travelled from hill to hill to see if she could see a
hoodie. She saw a hoodie on a hilltop but whenever
she got to the hill the hoodie would be in the
hollow: whenever she reached the hollow, the
hoodie would be on another hill.

When night came she had no place in which to
rest or stay. She saw a little house of light far from
her, but though it was far she did not take long to
reach it. She saw a little lad in the house and she
liked him very much. The woman of the house gave
her a bed for the night but no sooner had the day
come than she went out as usual. She passed this day
like the other days.

When night came she reached a house. The
woman of the house told her to come in, saying that

she knew the purpose of her journey. She told the girl that the hoodie, her husband, had only left the house a short while before and that as this was the last night she would see him, she was not to sleep but to strive and seize him. In this house she also saw a little lad whom she liked very much.

In spite of what the woman of the house had told her, she did fall asleep, and her husband came where she was, and let fall a ring on her right hand. When she awoke she tried to catch hold of him, and managed to seize a feather from his wing. He left the feather with her and flew away.

When she rose in the morning she didn't know what to do. The woman of the house told her that her husband had gone over the Hill of Poison across which she could not follow him unless she had horse-shoes on her hands and feet. She also gave her man's clothes, and told her to learn smithying until she was able to make horse-shoes for herself.

She learned smithying so well that she made horse-shoes for her hands and feet. She crossed over the Hill of Poison, and the day after she had done so she heard that her husband was to be married to the daughter of a great gentleman that was in the town.

There was a race in the town that day and everyone was to be at the race except the stranger that had come over Poison Hill. The cook came to her and asked her if she would go in his place to make the wedding feast, so that he might get to the race. She said that she would do so, and made a point of watching where the bridegroom would sit.

★　　★　　★

She let fall the ring and the feather in the broth that was in front of him. With the first spoon he took up the ring, with the next he took up the feather. When the minister came forward to carry out the wedding ceremony, the bridegroom would not marry till he had found out who had cooked the meal. They brought up the cook, and the bridegroom said that it was not he who had prepared the meal.

Then they brought up the one who had really prepared the meal and the bridegroom said that it was his wife. The spell vanished: and the two of them turned back over the Hill of Poison, she throwing the horse-shoes behind her as they went, and he following her.

When they had crossed the hill they went to the three houses in which she had been. They were the houses of her sisters, and they took away with them the three lads, for they were their own stolen sons. Then they returned to their own house and lived happily ever after.

Silver Weed

Honey under ground,
Silverweed of spring,
Honey and condiment,
Whisked whey of summer,
Honey and fruitage,
Carrot of autumn,
Honey and crunching,
Nuts of winter,
Between Feast of Andrew
and Christmastide.

The Cat

Creeping by night
Creeping by night
Creeping by night
  said the grey cat.

Creeping by night
With neither star nor gleam
Nor brightness, nor light
  said the grey cat.

The Goldfinch

'Beautiful yellow goldfinch
I will spend a Sunday
sweeping out your room,'
said the foolish yellow hen.

Serpent's Stone

This is a thing found among heather, especially old,
tall, unburnt heather. It is alleged that the serpent
goes round and round and round the clump of
heather emitting a froth or spittle from its mouth
upon the clump without stop or pause. No one
understands why this is. When the spittle emitted by
the serpent on the heather plant cools and dries, the
stuff grows as hard as a stone but as light as tinder.
The serpent's stone is about the size of a pullet's egg
and dark-grey in colour. Old people esteem it
highly for its power in healing and its power against
fairy women. It was good for swelling or cut or
bruise or festering in a person.

The Sea Maiden

There was once a fisherman who was very poor and
this particular year he wasn't catching much fish.
One day, when he was fishing, a sea maiden rose at
the side of his boat, and asked him if he was catching
much fish. The old man said that he was not.

'What reward will you give me for sending you
plenty of fish?' asked the sea maiden.

'Well,' said the old man, 'I haven't much to give
you.'

'Will you give me the first son you have?' she
asked.

'I would certainly give you that if I were to have
a son,' said the fisherman, 'but I haven't and won't
have a son, as my wife and I are grown so old.'

'Tell me everything you have,' said the sea
maiden.

'I have only an old mare, an old dog, myself and
my wife. These are all the creatures that belong to
me.'

'Here then,' said the sea maiden, 'are three grains
that you will give your wife this very night, three
more for the dog, three others for the mare, and
these last three you will plant behind your house and
in their own time your wife will have three sons,
your mare three foals, the dog three puppies, and
there will grow three trees behind your house, and
the trees will be a sign so that when one of your sons
dies one of the trees will wither. Now go home and
remember me when your son is three years of age
and you will get plenty of fish after this.'

Everything happened as the sea maiden said. His wife had three sons, his dog three puppies and his mare three foals: and the fisherman was catching plenty of fish. But when the end of the three years approached, the old man grew sorrowful and heavy-hearted because he was afraid of losing the son that the sea maiden had asked for. On the third anniversary of the day that he had met the sea maiden he went to fish as usual but he did not take his son with him.

The sea maiden rose at the side of the boat and asked, 'Did you bring your son to me?'

'No, I did not bring him,' said the old fisherman, 'I forgot that this was the day that I was supposed to bring him.'

'Well,' said the sea maiden, 'you may keep him for another four years to see if it will be easier for you to part with him. I have here a boy of the same age as him,' and she lifted up a big bouncing baby. 'Is your son as handsome as this one?'

The fisherman went home full of joy and delight because he had been allowed to keep his son for another four years and he kept on fishing and catching plenty of fish as before, but at the end of the four years he became sorrowful and heavy-hearted, and he would not take any food or do any work while his wife did not understand what was wrong with him.

He did not know what to do, but he determined that he would not take his son with him this time either. He went to fish as he had done in the past and the sea maiden rose at the side of the boat and asked him, 'Did you bring your son to me?'

'I forgot him this time too,' said the old man.

'Go home then,' said the sea maiden, 'and at the end of seven years after this you are sure to meet me but it will not be any easier for you to part with him then, either. However, you will get plenty of fish as you used to do.'

The old man went home full of joy for he had his son back for another seven years and before these seven years were up he thought that he himself would be dead and that he would not see the sea maiden any more. However this did not happen and the end of the seven years was approaching just as had happened before, and as before the old man was distressed with care and trouble. He couldn't rest by day or sleep by night.

One day the eldest son asked his father what it was that was troubling him. The old man admitted that something was but that he did not wish to talk about it. When the lad insisted that he must know, the father told him the story of what had happened between himself and the sea maiden.

'Don't let that trouble you,' said his son, 'I will not prevent you from carrying out your bargain.'

'No,' said his father, 'I will not let you go, even though I would not get any more fish.'

'If you will not let me go,' said his son, 'go to the blacksmith and ask him to make me a good strong sword and I will go and seek my fortune.'

His father went to the blacksmith who made a strong sword for him, but when he had taken the sword home and the lad had grasped it and given it a shake or two it broke into a hundred splinters.

He asked his father to go to the blacksmith again and get him another sword which would be twice as heavy as the first one: but when his father had done this and brought the sword back, it broke this time

into two halves. Back went the old man to the blacksmith and the smith made a great sword whose like he had never made before.

'There's your sword for you,' said the blacksmith, 'and the fist that clutches this sword must be strong.'

The old man gave the sword to his son who gave it a shake or two and said, 'This will do. It's high time for me to set out on my travels.'

Next morning the lad saddled the black horse that the mare had had, and running by his side was the black dog that the dog had had.

When he had travelled on a bit he came to the carcass of a sheep which was lying beside the road. Eating the carrion were a great dog, a falcon and an otter. He dismounted from the horse, and divided the carcass among the three of them, a share to the dog, a share to the otter and a share to the falcon.

'For this,' said the dog, 'if swiftness of foot or sharpness of tooth will help you, remember me, and I will be at your side.'

'For this,' said the otter, 'if swimming in a pool will help you, remember me, and I will be at your side.'

'For this,' said the falcon, 'if you are in trouble and swiftness of wing or the crook of a claw will help you, remember me, and I will be at your side.'

After this he went on till he reached a king's house, where he was given work as a herdsman, his wages to be according to the yield of milk that the cattle gave.

On the first day that he took the cattle out, the grazing was very bare and when evening came and he took them home they had not much milk, so that he was given very little food that night.

On the next day he took the cattle further and at last came to a very grassy place in a green glen, whose like he had never seen before.

But just when he was going to take the cattle home again after they had fed well, who should be seen coming towards him with a sword in his hand but a great giant.

'HIU, HAU, HOGARAICH,' shouted
the giant. 'It is a long time since my teeth were rusted
seeking your flesh. Your cattle are now mine for they
are on my land, and you are a dead man.'

'There is no knowing about that,' said the
herdsman, 'and it may be easier to say than to do.'

And so they came to grips, himself and the giant.
He drew the great clean-sweeping sword that the
smith had made for him, and approached his foe:
and as they were fighting his black dog leaped on
the giant's back. At that moment he drew back his
sword and cut the giant's head off.

Then he leaped on his black horse and went in

search of the giant's house. In his haste the giant had
left every gate and door open, and the herdsman
went in by a particular door and found the house
full of splendour of ornament and furniture, money
in plenty, and dresses of every kind of magnificent
richness in the wardrobe, and everything finer than
everything else. However he did not remove
anything from the giant's house, and at nightfall
went home again. That night when the cattle were
milked, there was a great rich flow, and he himself
was fed lavishly, and the king was greatly pleased
that he had found himself such a herdsman. So the
herdsman went to the green glen every day, but at
last the cattle had eaten it bare, and there was no
grass left.

The herdsman then thought that he would travel
a little further with them, and again he saw a great
grassy park. He returned for the cattle and set them
to feed there. They had only been grazing a little
time, when a great wild giant came towards him
full of rage and madness.

'HIU, HAU, HOGARAICH,' shouted the
giant. 'It is a drink of your blood that will
quench my thirst this night.'

'There is no knowing about that,' said the
herdsman, 'and it may be easier to say than to do.'

The two of them went at each other with much
flashing of sword blades, and it seemed that the giant
would gain the victory over the herdsman. However
he called on his black dog and with one spring it
caught the giant by the neck while the herdsman cut
off his head.

He went home very tired that night but again the herd yielded much milk and the whole family was delighted that they had such a good herdsman.

He continued to herd the cattle in this way for a long time but one night after he came home, instead of being greeted with delight and happiness he found that all were sad and sorrowful. He asked the dairymaid what was wrong and she told him that a great beast with three heads was in the loch, that someone was to be sacrificed to the beast every year, and that this year it was to be the king's daughter. 'Tomorrow at noon,' said the dairymaid, 'she is to meet the great monster at the upper end of the loch, but there is a great suitor who is going to rescue her.'

'What suitor is that?' asked the herdsman.

'Oh, he is as brave as a general,' said the dairymaid, 'and when he kills the beast he will marry the king's daughter, for the king has said that whoever saves his daughter will be allowed to marry her.'

On the following day as the time approached, the king's daughter and this heroic suitor went to meet the beast, and reached the black corrie at the upper end of the loch. They had been there only a short time when the beast stirred in the middle of the loch, and the suitor, terrified of the monster's appearance, ran away and hid himself. The king's daughter was left alone, frightened and trembling, for there was no one to rescue her.

Suddenly when she looked up she saw a brave handsome youth, riding a black horse, coming towards her. He was marvellously and splendidly arrayed, in full armour, and there was a black dog running after him.

'You look very wretched, girl,' said the youth. 'What are you doing here?'

'It doesn't matter,' replied the king's daughter. 'I won't be long here anyway.'

'I don't know about that,' said the youth.

'Someone as brave as you fled from here not so long ago,' said the king's daughter.

'One is only brave if one can stand up and fight,' said the youth.

He lay down beside her and told her that if he should fall asleep she should waken him when she saw the beast making for the shore.

'How will I waken you?' she said.

'I will tell you,' he said. 'You will waken me if you put the gold ring that is on your finger on my little finger.'

He had not been sleeping long when she saw the beast making for the shore. She took the ring off her finger and put it on the little finger of the lad who immediately woke up and went to meet the beast with his sword bared, and his dog running beside him.

What a spluttering and splashing there was in the loch, while the dog helped as well as he could and the king's daughter stood petrified on the shore. Now the beast and the youth would be under the water and now above it as they fought. Finally the youth succeeded in cutting off one of the monster's heads. The beast gave one huge roar which echoed

back from the rocks, stirred the loch into spindrift from end to end, and in a moment was out of sight.

'Good luck and victory were with you,' said the king's daughter. 'I am safe for one night but the beast will come again and again until the other two heads have been cut off.'

The youth caught the beast's head and drew a twisted twig through it, and he told her to bring it with her there tomorrow. She went home with the head on her shoulder, and the herdsman went back to his cattle. But the king's daughter had not gone far when the cowardly suitor saw her and told her that he would kill her if she did not say that it was he who had taken the head from the monster. As she was very frightened she agreed to say this and when they reached the king's house, the suitor was

carrying the head on his shoulder as if it was he who had cut it off. There was great rejoicing that the king's daughter should have come home alive, while the suitor held in his hand the beast's head which was stained with blood.

On the following day the two of them set off again, and there was no question at all but that the suitor would save the king's daughter. They reached the same place as before and they had not been there long when the fearful monster stirred in the middle of the loch, and the suitor ran away as he had done before, and as before the youth on the black horse arrived, this time wearing different but equally splendid armour.

'I am pleased to see you,' said the king's daughter. 'I hope that you will use your great sword as well as you did yesterday.'

Again the youth lay down beside her and said, 'If I sleep before the beast comes make sure that you waken me.'

'How will I waken you?' she asked.

'You will waken me,' he said, 'if you put the earring that is in your ear in mine.'

He had not been asleep long when the king's daughter cried, 'Waken up, waken up,' but the youth would not waken till she took the earring out of her ear and put it in his ear.

He woke immediately then and went to meet the
beast, and there was a huge spluttering and
splashing, while the beast roared and raved. They
fought for a long while – indeed, till it was nightfall
– when the youth succeeded in cutting another head
off the beast.

He put a twisted twig through it, leaped on his
black horse, and set off to look after his cattle, while
the king's daughter went home with the heads, the
one of the previous day and the one of that day.

When she was on her way home the suitor met
her, took the heads from her, and told her that she
must say that it was he who had cut the second head
off also. Again, because she was frightened, she
agreed to say this, and when they reached the king's
house with the heads there was great gladness and
joy. If the king had been hopeful that the suitor
would save his daughter, now he was even more
hopeful, and there was no question at all in his mind
that the third head would be cut from the beast on the
following day.

At the same time on the morrow the two set off,
and the suitor ran away and hid himself as he had
done previously.

The king's daughter went to the bank of the loch
and as before the hero with the black horse came
and lay down by her side. When the beast appeared
she woke him by putting an earring in his other ear,
and he and the monster began to fight. If the beast
had fought furiously on the previous occasions it
fought even more furiously now. But in spite of that
the hero cut off its third head after a long struggle.

He put a twisted twig through it as before, and the king's daughter went home with all three heads.

There was now great rejoicing in the palace, for the beast had finally been destroyed, and the suitor was to marry the king's daughter the following day. However, when the time of the wedding approached, and the guests were waiting for the priest to arrive to conduct the marriage, the king's daughter refused to marry anyone except the one who could take the heads off the twigs without cutting them.

'Who would take the heads off the twigs except the man who put them on?' said the king.

The suitor tried to remove them but he failed, and when everyone had tried, the king asked if there was anyone else who would be able to take them off.

Then it was remembered that the herdsman had not tried and word was sent for him and he did not take long to remove them

'Wait a minute,' said the king's daughter, 'the man who cut the heads off the beast has my ring and my two earrings.'

50

The herdsman put his hand into his pocket and
threw them on the table and the king's daughter
said, 'You are the man.'

The king was not very pleased when he saw that
it was a herdsman who was to marry his daughter
but he consented to the wedding, and ordered that
the herdsman should be better dressed. His daughter
said that she had something as fine as any that was in
the palace. The herdsman dressed and they were
married.

After the wedding they were as happy as could be
till one day when they were sauntering by the side
of the loch there came a beast even more fierce than
the first one and took the prince into the loch
without his being able to resist. The king's daughter
was blind with sorrow for her husband, and always
haunting the loch to see if she could find him. One
day she happened to meet an old blacksmith and
told him about her husband's fate. The smith
advised her to spread along the place from which
her husband had been seized all the fine things that
she could find, including her jewellery.

She waited till the beast appeared, and then when the beast said to her, 'Fine is your jewellery, king's daughter,' she replied, 'Finer than that is the jewel that you took away from me. Give me one sight of my husband and you shall have anything you like.'

The beast brought her husband to her and she said, 'If you release him you can take all that you see there.' The beast threw him alive and safe on the bank of the loch and took the jewellery and all the fine things that she had laid out.

A short time after this they were walking along the side of the loch again when the beast this time seized the king's daughter. The sorrow of everyone in the palace can be imagined, and her husband was sad and mournful, haunting the bank of the loch day and night. Again the old blacksmith met him as he had met his wife and told him that there was no way of killing the monster except to find the white-footed deer that was on the island in the middle of the loch. She was very fast and slender but when he had caught her a hoodie would spring out of her, and out of the hoodie a trout, and from the mouth of the trout an egg, but when the egg was broken the beast would be dead for its soul was in the egg.

O

Now as there was no way of getting to this island – for the beast would sink every boat or raft that would try to cross – he thought that he would leap the channel on his black horse with the black dog following him. After he had done this he saw the deer and let the black dog after her but she was so fast that when the dog was on one side of the island the deer was on the other.

'Oh,' said he, 'I wish that the dog that I met at the sheep's carcass were here.'

No sooner had he spoken than the dog was at his side and its speed was so great that it ran the deer to ground. When the deer had been caught a hoodie sprang out of her.

'Oh,' said he, 'I wish that the grey sharp-eyed swift-winged falcon that I met at the sheep's carcass were here.'

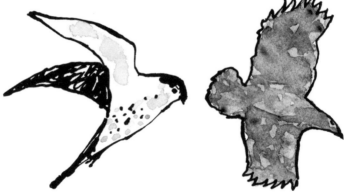

No sooner had he spoken than the falcon was in pursuit of the hoodie and it was not long in putting her to ground. As the hoodie fell on the bank of the loch the trout jumped out of her.

'Oh,' said he, 'I wish that the otter that I met at the sheep's carcass were here.'

No sooner had he spoken than the otter leaped
out of the loch and brought the trout to the bank.
As the egg sprang out of its mouth the prince put his
foot on it. The beast let out a roar and said, 'Do not
break the egg and you will get whatever you want.'

'I want you to release my wife,' said the prince,
and in the twinkling of an eye his wife was standing
by his side.

When he had caught her by the hand he put his
foot down on the egg and cracked it and the beast
died.

The two of them looked down at the horrifying
monster which was infested with hundreds of heads
and eyes and hundreds of feet. Then they went
home and there was great rejoicing in the king's
palace that night. The king honoured the prince
greatly and he was his favourite.

One day however when he and his wife were
walking beside the loch again the prince noticed a
little castle in a wood. When he asked his wife who

stayed in it she said that no one ever went near the
castle now, for whoever had gone near it had never
come back.

'I will go this very night to see who is staying in
it,' said the prince.

'Don't go,' she pleaded with him, 'for as I have
told you, no one has ever come back from that castle.'

'Be that as it may,' he replied, 'but I am going
there.'

And he went to the castle. When he knocked on
the door a little old woman came out and said
flatteringly, 'I am very pleased to see you. It is a
great honour to this kingdom that a man like you
should have come to it, and a greater honour still
that he should have visited my little hut. You go in
first, honoured one, and rest a little.' In he went but
as he did so she hit him on the head with her magic
wand and he fell down.

The next day there was sorrow in the king's
castle, for the prince didn't come back; and sorrow
too in the house of the prince's father, the fisherman
whom he had left so long ago, for the latter saw one
of the trees withering as had been foretold by the sea
maiden. The middle son told his father that the
eldest son must be dead, and swore that he himself
would go and find his body. He saddled the second
black horse and set off, the second black dog running
before him. Without straying from the road, he
followed his brother's tracks till he reached the king's
palace.

When he arrived they told him what had
happened, and how his elder brother had gone to

the castle in the wood. He too went to the castle as his brother had done, and it happened to him as it had happened to his brother. The old woman hit him on the head with the magic wand and he lay where he fell.

When the second tree withered the fisherman's youngest son said that now his two brothers were dead, he must find out what had happened to them. He saddled the third black horse and the third black dog went running ahead of them. He too arrived at the king's palace and they told him that his two brothers had gone to the castle in the wood. In spite of their pleadings he insisted that he too must go there, and when he reached the castle he was greeted as the others had been by the little old woman.

'I am very pleased to see you,' she told him. 'Go in and rest.'

This time however the youngest son said, 'You go in front of me, old woman. I don't like flattery. You go in and I'll hear what you have to say.'

In went the old woman and when her back was turned to him, he drew his sword and cut her head off. The sword flew out of his hands and the old woman clutched her head with both hands and put it back on her neck again. The black dog then sprang at the old woman and she hit it with the magic wand and it lay on the floor where it had been struck.

But the youth was not frightened and he came to grips with the evil old woman. He managed to grasp the magic wand and hit her on the head with it so hard that she fell on the ground in the twinkling of an eye.

He left her there and advancing into the house found his two brothers lying side by side. He hit each one with the magic wand and they immediately sprang to their feet, alive and well. And what gold and silver and other precious things they found in the old woman's castle! They took it away with them and went back to the king's palace where their safe return caused great rejoicing. As the king was growing old the fisherman's oldest son was crowned king. His two brothers stayed with him for a year and then went home carrying with them the treasure they had found in the old woman's castle as well as the presents that their brother gave them. And if there had been rejoicing in the king's palace, there was greater rejoicing in the poor fisherman's house because his sons were all well, and two of them had brought such great riches back.

The Dog

Dee do
said the white dog
   Dee do
said the white dog
   Dee do
Often were we
from night time till day
   happy and snug
said the white dog.

The Salmon Trout

O soft smooth salmon-trout
who took the butter from Ireland.
O soft white salmon-trout,
who took the cheese from Scotland!

The Speech of Birds

The mavis said:

Little red lad
Little red lad
   Come away home
   Come away home
   Come away home
My dear, to your dinner.

What shall I get?
What shall I get?
   A worm and a scrap of limpet!
   A worm and a scrap of limpet!
Hurry up! Hurry up!
   The night's coming!
   The night's coming!
And the darkness.

The Three Shirts

Once upon a time there was a king who had three sons and a daughter. Some time after his wife died he made up his mind that he would marry again, and his second wife got on well with the four children of his first.

One day however an evil witch came to see the queen and asked her how she and the king were getting on.

'We are getting on very well,' said the queen.

'And how are you getting on with the children?' asked the evil witch.

'Very well, too,' said the queen. 'I treat the children exactly as if they were my own.'

'Indeed,' said the evil witch, 'you are very foolish.'

'In what way?' asked the queen.

'Well,' said the evil witch, 'if the king were to die tomorrow your share of the inheritance wouldn't come to much.'

'God knows,' said the queen, 'that whatever happens to me I will not harm the children.'

'Oh,' said the evil witch, 'you don't need to do anything wrong. You just send them up to me and you will not be to blame for anything.'

'I don't know if I should do that,' said the queen.

But the evil witch kept on at her and finally said, 'You send them up to me tomorrow and tell them to ask for the yellow comb.'

The queen agreed to do this and the following day when the king was out as usual hunting in the

mountains she sent the oldest boy to the house of the
evil witch in order to get a yellow comb which he
was to bring back to her.

The poor lad went off suspecting nothing and
when he knocked on the door of the evil witch's
house she asked him to come in.

'What do you want, my dear?' she asked.

'My stepmother sent me,' he said, 'to get the
yellow comb.'

'It is over there on the dresser, my dear. Take it.'

He went across to the dresser to get the comb and
as he did so she lifted her magic wand and as he
picked up the comb she struck him with it and he
was changed into a black raven. He turned and went
out of the house and as he was crossing the threshold
he spat out a mouthful of blood and flew away.

When there was no sign of him coming back, his
stepmother said to the second oldest boy, 'You had
better go and see where your brother is and tell him
to come home. If you do not see him, ask for the
yellow comb.'

The second brother then set off and when the first
brother, who had been turned into a raven, saw him
coming he began to dart at his head as if trying to
warn him. What the second brother did however
was to run as fast as he could to get to the shelter of
the evil witch's house before the raven could harm
him.

When he had got inside he asked her, 'Has my
brother been here?'

'O, no, my dear,' she said.

'Well,' he said, 'he was supposed to come here

for the yellow comb. My stepmother sent him.'

'He has not been here at all,' said the evil witch, 'but there is the yellow comb on the dresser and you can take it.'

The poor boy went over to get the comb but when he had almost reached it the evil witch changed him with her magic wand into a black raven. He flew out of the house as his older brother had done, and as he went he saw the blood at the door and he too spat out a mouthful of blood beside it.

When the two brothers had not come back, the stepmother sent the third brother to the evil witch's house with the same instructions, and as he was approaching it he was attacked by the two ravens who darted at him trying to prevent him from going forward and so fierce was their squawking that it seemed as if they were almost talking. But he did the same as the second brother had done and ran into the house of the evil witch for shelter. When he had got inside he asked her, 'Were my two brothers here?'

'No indeed,' she said, 'none of your brothers was here. Were they supposed to be coming here?'

'Yes,' said the third brother, 'my stepmother sent them to get the yellow comb.'

'O, none of them has been here,' she said, 'but the comb is over there on the dresser and you can go across and take it.'

The poor boy went across and, as had happened to the other two, when he was going to pick up the yellow comb he was struck by the wand and

changed into a black raven. He flew out and joined
the other two, leaving a mouthful of blood at the
door.

Finally, anxious about the disappearance of the
three brothers, the stepmother sent the girl saying,
'Goodness, you had better see what has happened to
your brothers. Everyone is going and no one is
coming back.'

So the girl went and when they saw their sister
coming the three brothers who had been changed
into ravens set about her, darting round her head
and trying to drive her back. Before she got to the
house it struck her that something was wrong and
when she reached the door she noticed the three
mouthfuls of blood on the threshold. When she

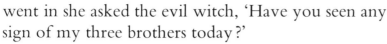

went in she asked the evil witch, 'Have you seen any sign of my three brothers today?'

'No, my dear,' she said.

'Are you sure you have not?' said the girl.

'No, indeed,' said the witch.

'Well,' said the girl, 'my stepmother sent them up to get the yellow comb.'

'They have certainly not been here,' said the evil witch, 'but the yellow comb is over there on the dresser and you can go across and take it.'

The girl went but as she was going she kept an eye on the woman who was behind her, and when she saw her lifting the magic wand she sprang at her and seized the wand and struck the witch with it on the top of her head and turned her into a pillar of stone.

'You can stay there,' she said, turning and going out and leaving the comb where it was. As she was crossing the threshold she noticed the three mouthfuls of blood and gathered them in her handkerchief. When she left the house it was almost nightfall and the three ravens were diving about her for joy that she had escaped safely.

The ravens headed south and she followed them on foot but as the darkness fell she could only follow them by their croaking in the sky above her. Finally however she lost them and as she looked around her she saw a light towards which she walked. The light was from a house but when she knocked at the door there was no reply, so she opened the door and went in and sat down. She waited to see if anyone would come but no one came. Then she heard the ravens croaking and coming towards the house. They flew in and sat at the table.

'Well,' said they, 'you got away with your life.'

'Yes,' she replied.

As there was food on the table they had a meal and after they had eaten she said to them,

'Is there anything in the world that can break the spell that binds you?'

'Yes, there is one thing,' said the oldest one, 'but I don't suppose you can do it.'

'Let me hear what it is then.'

'Well, it's this,' he answered, 'You must make a shirt of bog cotton for each one of us and from the day that you begin to pick the bog cotton to the day when you say, "Health to wear your shirt, sweet brother," you must not utter one single solitary word.'

'We will see what can be done,' she said.

When daylight came they flew off and when she had put the house in order she set off to the hills and began to pick bog cotton. She picked a sackful that day and after leaving it where she had picked it she returned to the house and waited there till her raven brothers came in. They immediately tried to catch her out and make her speak but they did not get a single word from her all night long.

Next morning they flew away again and she herself went to the hills as before, after she had set the house in order, and picked another sackful that day. She placed it beside the one she had picked the previous day and returned to the house. Again they tried to catch her out but she would not speak a word.

Next morning they flew off again, and she left the house earlier than usual to see if she could pick a sackful of bog cotton and carry it nearer the road. All day she picked and in the evening, before it had grown dark, she thought that she would start to carry the sacks to the road. By the time she had brought the sacks there it had got dark, so dark that she could not make out which way she ought to go in order to find the house again. Then it occurred to her that if she went back to the house her brothers would only be tormenting her anyway, trying to get her to speak, and she decided that she would wait in the shelter of the sacks until it was daylight and she could see where she was going.

This then was what she did and she stayed in the shelter of the sacks at the roadside. Suddenly as she waited there she heard the hoofbeats of a horse and saw a horseman coming. The man passed her and then, as if sensing something, stopped. He looked

and thought he saw something that was not usually at the side of the road. So he dismounted and went across and found her beside the sacks. When he spoke to her she didn't answer, and no matter how many questions he put to her she didn't answer. Finally, he went and lifted her up and set her behind him on the horse and off the two of them went. When he came to his own house he lifted her down from the horse, and brought her into the house where there was no one but his mother and himself. He was in fact a great gentleman and his house was fine and splendid.

He told his mother how he had found the girl at the side of the road beside the sacks, and that he would have to bring the sacks home for her. That night she slept in the gentleman's house, and in the morning he went to fetch her sacks and bring them home. When she had got her sacks she set to work at the bog cotton, carding it and spinning it with a distaff.

Time passed, and the gentleman grew fond of her, and finally they were married. But nothing would take her away from her shirts at which she worked all the time.

The night before the birth of her first child she had finished the first shirt, folded it, and put it in a locker that she had in her room. She then gave birth to a baby boy but in the morning he had disappeared. As she was dumb no one could get any answer to the questions that were asked, and it was even suggested to the gentleman that she herself had killed the child.

'There is no saying what has happened,' said the gentleman, 'and we will wait and see.' For the girl was very beautiful and he loved her.

Still she worked at the shirts and when she had recovered from the birth of her first child, who had been stolen away so mysteriously, she started to card and comb and spin the second shirt.

The time came when she expected her second child and before it was born she folded the second shirt and put it away with the first one. Despite all the precautions that were taken, the second child – another boy – was also stolen. Again it was suggested to the gentleman that his wife must be the one who was killing the children but again he answered, 'There is no saying what has happened. We shall wait and see.' There was also gossip that she was clearly not normal for she did not speak a word though she worked hard all the time.

When she had recovered from the birth of the second child she began on the third shirt, carding and combing and spinning.

Time passed and she was expecting her third child and the night before his birth – for he was another boy – she folded the third shirt and put it away in the locker along with the first two. In the morning they found that the boy who had been born had disappeared like the first two. Again it was suggested to the gentleman that it must be his wife who was killing the children and so great was the anger and uproar that it was decided that she should be burnt, for she was clearly unnatural in any case because she never spoke a word to anyone. A great crowd

gathered at the place where she was going to be burnt, and just when it was time for her to be brought out, three horsemen were seen approaching.

The gentleman asked the people to wait a moment and when the three horsemen came up, the first one was carrying in front of him a boy about three years old, the second one was carrying a boy about two years old, and the last one was carrying a baby.

The first one, who was carrying the oldest child, dismounted and said, 'What is the meaning of all this?' The gentleman told him what had happened, and how his wife was being blamed for the disappearance of the three children.

'May I and my two brothers here speak to this girl?' said the first one.

'Indeed you may,' said the gentleman. 'You may have a word with her, and you may take her away if you wish, for I do not wish to see her burned. Come in here.'

And he took them all to the girl's room – that is, the girl, the three brothers and the three children – and he remained outside while the brothers locked the door.

The girl then went across to her locker and took out the first shirt she had made and she gave it to the eldest brother for him to try it on. When he had put it on, she said, 'Health to wear your shirt, sweet brother.'

'Good health to you, sister,' he replied, 'and here is your first child.' The gentleman, who was standing outside the door, demanded that it be opened when he heard his wife speaking but he was told by the brothers that it was not to be opened yet.

The girl went to the locker and brought out the second shirt and gave it to the next brother to put on. When he had dressed himself in it, she said, 'Health to wear your shirt, sweet brother,' and he replied, 'Good health to you, sweet sister, and here is your second son.'

The gentleman, who was standing outside, again demanded that the door be opened when he heard his wife speaking, but the brothers would not open it. He put his shoulder to the door and burst through it and said to his wife, 'You are certainly not going away, now that I have heard you speak.'

His wife asked him to stand back for a moment till she had given the third brother his shirt, which she took from the locker.

'Health to wear your shirt, sweet brother,' she said, and he answered, 'Good health to you, sweet sister, and here is your baby.'

She took the child and held it and all that now remained to be done was to clear away the crowd that had gathered to see her burnt.

Her brothers stayed with her husband, his mother and herself, and the three children, for her husband was a rich man: and they were all very happy together.

Fables

The hoodie and the fox were good at getting up early in the morning, and they laid a bet with each other as to who was the earlier riser. The hoodie went into a tree-top and slept there: and the fox stayed at the foot of the tree looking upward to see when the day would come. As soon as he saw the daylight appearing he shouted out, 'It is bright day now.'

The hoodie who had slept all night awoke with a cry and answered, 'It's been bright day for some time now.' So the fox lost his bet and the hoodie won it.

One day the fox succeeded in catching a fine fat
goose asleep by the side of a loch. He held her by the
wing and making a joke of her cackling, hissing and
fears he said:

'Now if you had me in your mouth as I have you,
tell me what you would do.'

'Why,' said the goose, 'that is an easy question. I
would fold my hands, shut my eyes, say a grace and
then eat you.'

'Just what I mean to do,' said the fox and folding
his hands and looking very demure he said a pious
grace with his eyes shut.

But while he did this the goose had spread her
wings and was half way across the loch: so the fox
was left to lick his lips for his supper.

'I will make a rule of this,' he said in disgust,
'never in my life to say grace again till I have the
meat warm in my belly.'

76

The Seal Woman

Once upon a time there was a man called
MacCodrum, and he used to go beachcombing. He
would walk along the shore to see if he could find
seaweed which he would use as manure for his
crops: or he might find pieces of timber, which had
been washed ashore from wrecked ships, sometimes
with iron bolts attached to them which he could use
for his barn.

One day when he was beachcombing as usual he
decided he would take a rest and did so in the shelter
of a rock. As he was sitting there looking out into
the bay what did he see but a group of seals making
their way towards the beach. He watched them as
they dragged themselves up to the bank. But what
was strangest of all, when they reached the bank, they
took off their skins and changed into beautiful women.
Then they left their skins on the bank and went
out to sea again, swimming and playing in the water.

As he watched in fascination, MacCodrum
noticed that one of the seal women was more
beautiful than the rest, though they were all pretty
enough. The skin that she had been wearing, and
which she had left behind as the others had done,
was also prettier than the skins of the other seals, and
he looked from the skin to the woman and back
again for a long time.

MacCodrum had never in his life seen any
woman as beautiful as this, and so beautiful was she
that he fell in love with her as she swam and played
in the water.

'I will take her skin,' he thought, 'and perhaps she will follow me and not go back to the sea again.' No sooner had he thought of this than he went quickly to get the skin before the beautiful seal woman came back. At that moment all the seals noticed him and made for the shore as fast as they could but he managed to seize the beautiful woman's skin before she arrived. He thrust it under his arm while the other seals took their own skins and swam out to sea again and were lost to sight.

But the woman whose skin he was holding did not leave as the others did. She wept and pleaded with him to give her the skin back so that she could rejoin her companions. But MacCodrum, who was dazzled by her beauty, would not give the skin back in case he lost her forever.

'No,' said MacCodrum, 'this skin is too beautiful for me to give it away again. I am going to keep it.' His heart was almost breaking with the pleadings that the seal woman made but he thought that the worst thing that could ever happen to him was to lose her, and so he made his way home, looking back to see if the woman was following him. And she did follow him, still pleading for her sealskin.

'I must not lose this skin,' said MacCodrum to himself, 'or she will leave me and go back to the sea again. I must hide it very carefully.' And so he hid it behind the rafters in the barn, making sure that the seal woman was not looking.

'What shall I do?' said the seal woman. 'What shall I do? I have no home on land or sea.'

'You may stay with me,' said MacCodrum.

'I will marry you and give you a home.'

Still the seal woman pleaded with him for her skin but MacCodrum, who loved her greatly and did not want to lose her, refused to give it to her.

'Since I have no home now on land or sea,' said the seal woman at last, 'I will marry you.'

And so they did get married and lived happily together for MacCodrum who loved her deeply was good to her, but often the seal woman would fall into a dream as if she were still thinking of her home in the sea to which, if she could, she would return.

As MacCodrum loved his seal wife more and more deeply it worried him that perhaps she might find the skin and leave him. He therefore decided that he would take it from behind the rafters in the barn and put it into a cornstack which he built every harvest time. When the corn was taken in he would

put the skin behind the rafters again till the next
cornstack was built, when he would hide the skin in
it once more. He always left that stack as the last that
he brought into the barn every spring.

Year after year passed like this and it seemed that
the seal woman had forgotten about her home in the
sea, for she was an excellent wife and a good mother
to the children that they now had.

One particular year however when MacCodrum
was getting the cornstack into the barn in the spring,
some of the children were helping him with the
work. He managed to get the skin out of the stack
and hid it behind the rafters in the barn till he built
the next stack.

However that night when the seal woman was putting
her children to bed, the youngest girl said to her:

'Oh, mother, what a beautiful thing father had in
the stack today.'

'What was that, darling?' said her mother.

'It was a fur coat,' said the girl, 'as beautiful as you
ever saw.'

'Could you tell me, darling, where he put it?' said
her mother.

'He hid it behind the rafters in the barn,' said the girl.

'Well, then,' said the seal woman, 'I'm now going
to leave you for a little while but I'll come back
again, and you won't be short of fish. You keep a
look-out for me.'

The seal woman stayed for a long while thinking,
after she had left her children, for her heart was
almost breaking between the desire for the sea and
the love of them, but as she looked out into the

moonlit bay she saw the seals sporting in the water, the moonlight flashing off their backs, and she seemed to hear them calling to her. She went to find the skin where her husband had left it, and she put it on, and soon she was out in the water again.

When her husband missed the skin, for he went very often to see if it was still there, and when his wife was not to be found anywhere, he asked his children if they knew what had happened. They told him, and he realized that his wife had gone back to the sea from which she could not bear to be parted.

Many times he would go down to the shore to look for her, and sometimes he would see a seal with a fish in its mouth which it would leave on the shore for him to find. It would make a sound like crying and he knew that this was his wife leaving food for her children.

'I forgive you,' he said. 'I should not have taken you from the sea to which you belonged. It was my fault.' But day after day the seal would come with the fish and he knew that the seal woman had forgotten neither him nor his children. He told the children that their mother would come back some day, and he sometimes believed that this would happen, for she never forgot them and would always bring a fish for their food: sometimes too it seemed that she was singing to them as she had done when they were small.

The Brown Bear of the Green Glen

There was a king once who had three sons. John was the name of the youngest one and it was said that he was rather foolish and simple. Now this king lost his sight and the strength of his feet, and the two elder brothers said that in order to cure him they would go and seek three bottles of the water of the Green Isle that was in the middle of the sea: and so they went away on that quest.

The fool then said that he would go away as well: but in the first town that he reached in his father's kingdom, whom should he see there but his two brothers.

'Oh,' he said, 'so you are here.'

'Get home,' they told him, 'as quickly as possible or we will take your life.'

'Don't worry, lads,' said John, 'I don't want to stay with you.'

So John rode away till he came to a great waste wood. 'Hoo hoo,' said John to himself, 'it is not wise for me to travel this wood alone,' for night was falling and it was growing dark.

John tied the lame white horse that he was riding to the root of a tree and he climbed up into the top himself. He had only been there for a short time when he saw a bear coming towards him with a fiery cinder in its mouth.

'Come down, king's son,' said the bear.

'Indeed I won't,' said John, 'I think I am safer where I am.'

'If you will not come down, I will go up,' said the bear.

'Do you take me for a fool?' said John. 'A shaggy shambling creature like you to climb a tree!'

'If you will not come down, I will go up,' said the bear as he began to climb the tree.

'It is true you can climb right enough,' said John. 'Keep back from the tree and I will climb down and talk to you.'

And when he had climbed down he and the bear began to chat. When the bear asked him if he was hungry John said that he was, a little, and the bear set off and came back with a roebuck that he had caught.

He roasted the meat and after they had eaten, he told John, 'Lie down between my paws and you will have no cause to fear cold or hunger till morning.'

Early in the morning the bear asked, 'Are you asleep, king's son?'

'I am not sleeping very heavily,' said John.

'Well,' said the bear, 'it is time for you to be off. But are you a good horseman, John? Your journey is a long one – two hundred miles.'

'There are worse horsemen than me,' said John.

'Then you had better leave your horse behind you and climb on my back,' said the bear.

John tried to do this but when he made his first leap he fell to the ground.

'Well, well,' said John, 'I had better try again.' And with his nails and his feet he clung to the bear's back till they reached the end of the two hundred miles and a giant's house.

'Now, John,' said the bear, 'you will pass the night in this giant's house. You will find him pretty grumpy but tell him that it was the brown bear of the green glen that left you here for the night, and I am sure that you will get a good welcome.'

So John left the bear and went to the giant's
house.

'King's son,' said the giant, 'it was foretold that
you would come: and if I never managed to catch
hold of your father I have at least got his son. I don't
know whether I should stamp you into the earth
with my feet or blow you into the sky with my
breath.'

'You won't do either of these,' said John, 'for it
was the brown bear of the green glen that left me
here.'

'Come in then, king's son,' said the giant, 'and
you will be looked after well this night.'

And he was true to his word for John was given
plenty of food and drink. The following day the
bear took John to another giant.

'Now,' said the bear, 'I don't have much acquaintance with this giant, but you will not be long in his house before you will have to wrestle with him, and if he is too strong for you, you must say, "If I had the brown bear of the green glen here he would soon master you".'

As soon as John went into the giant's house, the giant cried, 'Ai ai, ee ee. If I did not catch your father, I have certainly got his son,' and he began to wrestle with him.

They wrestled so fiercely that they made the hardest rock soft and in the softest places they sank up to their thighs: and the giant gave John a sore wrench or two.

At last John shouted, 'If I had the brown bear of the green glen here he would soon master you.'

And no sooner had he spoken than the bear was at his side.

Then the giant said to John, 'King's son, now I know what must be done as well as you know it yourself.'

And he ordered his shepherd to bring home the best sheep that was on the hill and to throw its carcass in front of the great door.

'Now, John,' said the giant, 'an eagle will come and settle on the carcass of this sheep and there is a wart on the ear of this eagle which you must cut off with this sword without drawing a drop of blood.'

The eagle came but it had not been eating the carcass long when John drew close to it and with one stroke of the sword he cut off the wart without shedding one drop of blood.

'Now,' said the eagle, 'climb on the root of my two wings, for I know what is to be done better than you know it yourself.'

John did as he was told and they flew over land and sea till they reached the Green Isle.

'Now John,' said the eagle, 'be quick and fill the three bottles.'

After he had filled the bottles with water out of the well, John saw a little house beside him and decided to go in and see what it was like.

In the first room that he entered he saw a full bottle. He filled a glass out of it and drank it but when he was leaving he looked behind him and saw that the bottle was as full as it had been before. 'I will have this strange bottle along with my three bottles of water,' he said to himself.

Then he went into another room and saw a loaf. He took a slice out of it and saw that the loaf was as whole as it had been before. 'I will have this loaf along with the rest,' he said to himself.

Then he went into another room and saw a cheese which remained whole after he had taken a slice from it. He decided that he would take the cheese as well.

Finally he went into another room and saw there the prettiest girl he had ever seen. 'It would be a great pity not to kiss your lips, my dear,' said John.

He kissed her but no sooner had he done so than he had to climb on the eagle's back for his return journey. The eagle took him on the same path that they had taken before, till they reached the giant's house, where at this time his tenants were paying their rent to him, and there was a feast with a great deal of food and drink.

'Well, John,' said the giant, 'did you ever see such drink as I have here, in your father's house?'

'Pooh,' said John, 'I have a drink that is unlike yours and much better.' And he gave the giant a drink out of the bottle that he had found in the house where the girl was.

'Well,' said the giant, 'I will give you two hundred pounds and a bridle and a saddle for this bottle.'

'It's a bargain then, but I have also got a loaf better than you have ever tasted.' And he offered it to the giant who took a taste and said,

'I will give you two hundred pounds and a bridle and a saddle for this as well.'

'But that is not all,' said John, 'I have here a cheese
which is the best cheese you have ever tasted.'

And again the giant took a taste of the cheese and
said,

'I will give you two hundred pounds and a
bridle and a saddle for this as well.'

'It's a bargain,' said John. 'But the first sweetheart
that I ever kissed must get them if she calls for
them.' He was thinking of the girl whom he had
kissed in the house that was on the Green Isle.

The giant agreed to these terms, and John set off
to his father's kingdom, and met his two brothers on
the way.

'You had better come with me,' he told them,
'and you will get a saddle and a bridle and two
hundred pounds each.'

The two brothers followed him but when they
were near their father's house they thought they had
better kill him as it was he who had succeeded in
getting the three bottles of water to cure their father
of his sickness. So they attacked him and when they
thought he was dead they threw him behind a dike
and they took the three bottles of water and went
home.

John had not been lying long in the ditch when
his father's blacksmith came that way with a
cartload of rusty iron. John called out that whoever
was passing should help him if he was at all a
Christian. The blacksmith lifted him up and threw
him among the iron, and because the iron was so
rusty it went into each wound that John had, and
caused him to become rough-skinned and bald.

Now the girl whom John had left in the Green Isle had fallen in love with him and could not forget him, even though she had seen him for such a short time, and she decided to try and find him. She went for advice to an old woman who told her, 'I have a bird here and as soon as he sees your sweetheart he will hop on top of his head.' The Green Isle was searched from end to end to see if the bird would settle on the head of any of the young men, but it did not stir, and the girl's sweetheart John was not to be found.

'Well,' said the girl to the bird, 'we will travel through the world together till we find my sweetheart.'

Eventually she came to the house of the giant and she saw the bottle.

'Ai, ai,' said she to the giant, 'and who gave you this bottle?'

'It was young John, the king's son,' said the giant, 'that left it.'

'But I tell you that the bottle is mine,' said the girl.

When she noticed the loaf she asked the giant where he had got it and he gave her the same answer as before. And so it was with the cheese, as well.

'I will take the bottle and the loaf and the cheese,' said the girl, and the giant agreed to let her take them, according to the promise he had made to John.

So the girl made her way to the king's palace where all the young men and young women of the country were gathered for a feast.

She asked to see all the young men, and they were
all passed before her, but the bird did not stir.

Then she asked if there was anyone else from
among the young men of the country who wasn't
there at the feast.

'I have a bald rough-skinned lad in the smithy,'
said the blacksmith. 'But . . .' And he shook his head.

'Rough-skinned or not,' she said, 'you go and
send him here.'

No sooner did the bird see the head of the bald
rough-skinned lad than it settled on top of it. The
girl caught the lad and kissed him and said, 'You are
my sweetheart.' And immediately he was changed
into the handsome young man he had been.

So John married the girl who was really the
daughter of the King of the Green Isle and they
had a great wedding that lasted for seven days and
they were happy ever after.

The Calfless Cow or
The Cow Without a Calf

'Leap the dyke', is the calfless cow,
trouble of neighbours is the calfless cow,
curse of herdsman the calfless cow,
head to rocky ground the calfless cow.

A useless head is the calfless cow,
a head of mischief is the calfless cow,
no shapely form has the calfless cow,
no increase has the calfless cow.

Head on high is the calfless cow,
head without triumph is the calfless cow,
worst of the byre is the calfless cow,
worst of the herd is the calfless cow.

Lullaby

You are not the round–headed seal's blue cub,
You are not the seagull's grey chick,
You are not the otter's crooked whelp,
You are not the lean cow's puny calf.

se: TM 8582